Life Hack!

Unlock the key to Happiness, tap into your true potential, and success will follow.

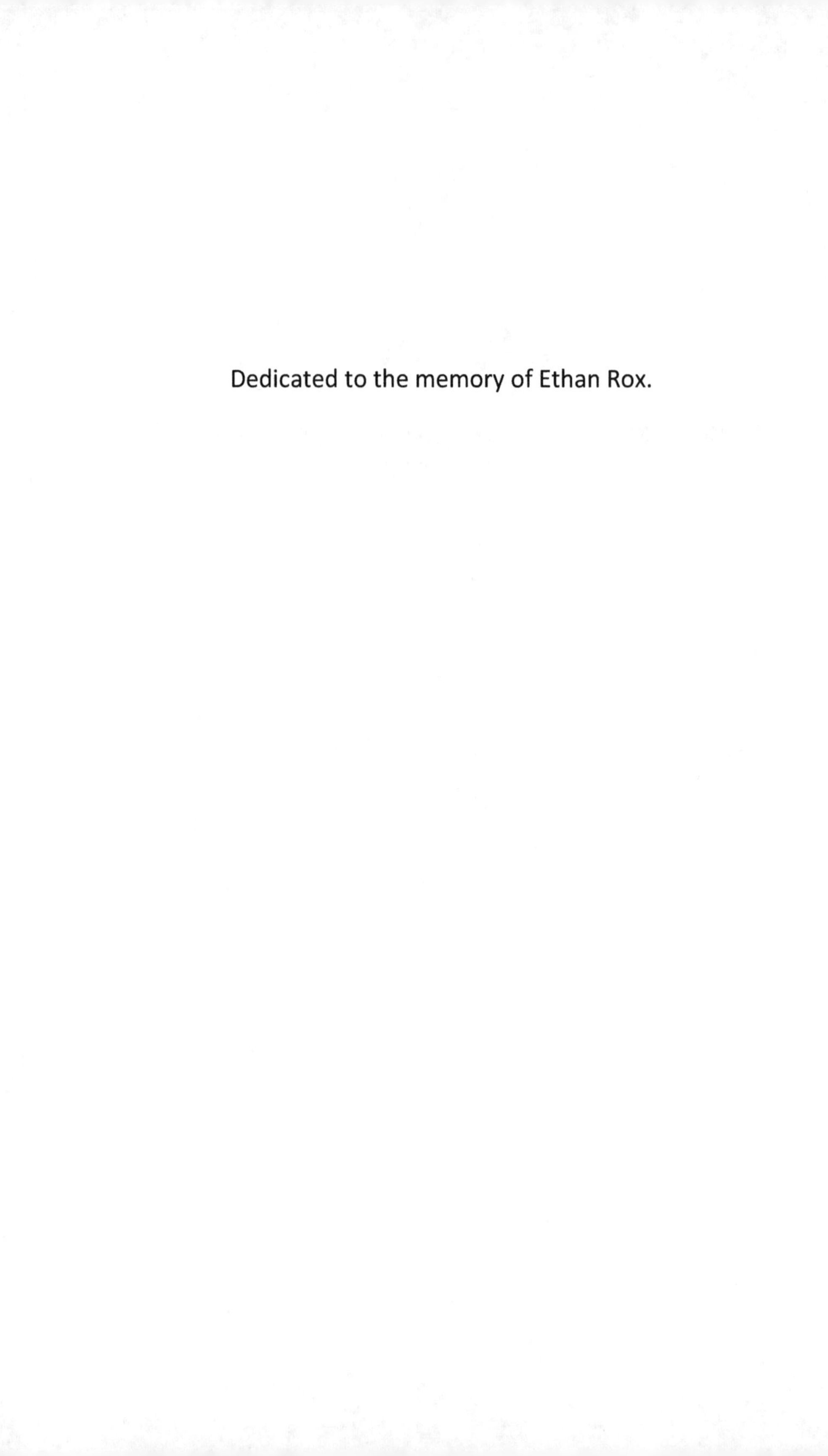

Dedicated to the memory of Ethan Rox.

Preface

Some handbooks may be referred to as self-help books, but I refer
to mine as a self-discovery book. I practice what I preach and want
you to tap into your TRUE POTENTIAL. I wrote this in six months,
but it was really 44 years in the making. Some of my thoughts may
be redundant and you may think "yeah no kidding guy, that's
common sense." But I think once you are more mindful of these
ideas and practices, you will add them to your bag of tools, and
change your life!

My motivation to write this handbook is to share some LIFE
CHANGING practices to help younger generations and to tell my
story. Here are four main reasons. First, summer 2019, out of the
blue I found out I had 3 tumors on my spleen. For months I worried
myself sick not knowing if it was cancer. I was in a lot of pain and
mentally already grieving my own demise. I made all the
preparations: updated my will, possessions distributed, got my cat a
good home, etc. After months of tests and waiting for the news, my
doctor told me he believes the tumors are benign. Sigh of relief. I

promised myself if I was not taking a ride on the Spirit Horse then I will be living life to the fullest and try to make the world a better place. I have a follow up MRI in two weeks from now.

Second, in February of 2019, one of my dearest friends and former band mates committed suicide. He was like a brother to me and was always there for me. It broke my heart into a thousand pieces that I was not there for him. About five years ago I went through a bad break up. The girl of my dreams left me the day she was supposed to move in with me. I was devastated. I never felt so alone and hurt in my life. I called my friend and he calmed me down. Meanwhile he was going through an awful divorce and was battling his own demons. "Ryan, my phone is always by me. Call me anytime. I don't care if it's the middle of the night, let it rip!" I believe he saved my life then and maybe now too. From his death I started a new path. Sobriety. Or at least limited drinking and the end of binge drinking for so many years. Balance is key. As he used to say during rehearsal, "I am laser focused." He was a master of his craft. I miss him always.

The third reason for writing this is COVID-19. In April of 2020 I got sick. I was ill for about 4 or 5 weeks. It was brutal. Fatigue and non-stop flu symptoms. My Teladoc doctor believed I had the Corona virus. There were nights I had heavy chest pain and fevers. I convinced myself I would beat it, or I would join my recently deceased friend. I didn't care anymore. About day 24 in self-quarantine I thought I broke. But then day 85 came and passed. When I was healthy again, my spirit was renewed and had a new appreciation for life. My dear band mate, Veronica, and I wrote some deep hearted material. Another rebirth in my life.

Finally, my fourth reason is I want the underdog to have a leg up in life. My high school guidance counselor told me I would never amount to anything. I did not have any focus. I was a bit of a degenerate. But he mainly criticized me because I was a dreamer. Worse counselor of the world award goes to... :) It wasn't until later in my adult life that I realized ADHD was an extreme challenge. I opted to never go on meds. I saw the effects on a fellow creative and watched his art flow STOP. I'd rather muscle through it and find my path.

Once I went to college and discovered martial arts, I was changed forever. It laid the groundwork for the rest of my life. It gave me focus, discipline, and confidence. It helped in all aspects of my life: hockey, problem solving, and more. The common denominator of most of this handbook derives from the Okinawan discipline of Isshin Ryu karate and the philosophy of Buddhism. The way of the warrior. The present is now, the past is dead, and the future can wait. And, the Golden Rules. But still, I am a student of life. Each day a new beginning.

Ryan Phoenix

Bay Village, OH

7.19.20

About the author of Life Hack!

Ryan Phoenix grew up in Cleveland, OH from a middle-class family. As a youth he was a degenerate with bad grades and no clear focus. He struggled to get into college but finally did and there he discovered martial arts. He learned to respect authority and self-discipline. After graduating college, he struggled with survival jobs for a few years and then landed a corporate job. He also played in bands and eventually became an actor and traveled often. All the while investing heavily since he was 23 years old in the Fortune 500 company he still works for. In the next 9 to 10 years he will retire a multi-millionaire. Currently he is writing handbooks like Life Hack! His goal, to help send the elevator back up and inform other trouble youths that they can achieve great things!

Chapters:

Welcome to Life Hack! The NEW college is learning on the job of LIFE! At the end of this handbook please do not hesitate to book me through my Facebook page, Ryan's Mind, Body, & Soul Consulting to go deeper on any of these chapters.

Set Routine.

Choose the tone of your day on your terms!

Mix it Up.

BreakFAST

Limitations.

Metrics is not just for Nerds.

Meditation

Zen in ALL Things

Stay Positive

Listen to the Universe

Friends

Three Deep Breathes.

The Balance of Extremes.

Learn Survival Skills.

Travel!

Procrastination is Your Dream Killer.

Mantra.

Porn = the Death of your Relationship
Exercise More.

Take an Acting Class.

Stop Comparing Yourself to Others.

No Excuses.

Recognize and Stop Distractions.

Cut Off Toxic People!

Show Them, Don't Tell Them.

Watch More Documentaries *(The Minimalists)*

A Smoothie a Day!

Recognize your Addictions!

Power Naps.

Use apps for Time Management: Time is your biggest asset

Decision Making: + and – T chart.

Stop Clock Watch at your 9 to 5 Job

Wake up 3 hours before the day job.

Daily practice of Mind, Body, Soul.

Recognize when you need Mini Breaks from the Hustle.

The Haters: Kill them with Kindness.

Decide what you need to Sacrifice in your life to free up TIME.

Have a "spa day."

The Lazy Investor Portfolio

Set Strict Deadlines

Stop Waiting in Lines
Compete with Yourself not with Friends nor Family.

Mix Things Up.

Beware of FEAR and GREED.

Don't Aim for the Fence, Aim for the parking lot!

Some Days You're the bug, some days you're the windshield.

Pay It Back.

The Value of Kindness and Integrity.

Choose Your Mentors Wisely.

Life is Like Walking on a Tight Rope.

Set Routine.

Six months ago, during the pandemic I started going to bed at 10pm and waking up at 6am every day. I really wanted to change my routine but had no idea the Universe would force it upon me. Thanks pandemic?! I wanted to get more quality sleep and more time before my day job to write, garden, and exercise. This may sound kind of robotic, but I think it's pretty sound advice. Drink a full glass of water upon waking up. It rehydrates the body after sleep and helps digestion. No social media nor non-business texts nor emails. This first 30 minutes is for you. Stillness in your mind, body, and spirit is key. This is your time. A calm before the day's hustle. Set the tone of the day on your terms. The whole point of this handbook is to find balance daily. Creating healthy habits that become the fabric of your being.

Each morning (summer and spring) on my property, I pick up leaves, branches, and water my plants. Zen gardening (soul). Then I read the Wall Street Journal (mind). Lastly, I take a walk to the lake (body). And when I get to the lake and take a gander, I take in three deep breaths and feel the chi flowing (soul). When you start to find what works for you, your life will change, and you will feel the balance and fulfilment. It's simple and most things balanced revolve around the number three.

Take a tree for example. Rooted to the Earth. It's body above the ground and it branches into the sky. Real "OG" balance there! When you are balanced, your feet are rooted to the Earth, your body the tree, and your head floating like a balloon. Your imagination in the clouds for big visions you have for the future! Or it is simply focused on cleaning up some cat litter or a school supply list you need to write. Zen in all things.

Choose the Tone of the Day on Your Terms

Some days it seems like the moment you wake up the Universe is ready to challenge you. Neighbor's dog barking at 4am. Maybe a bad dream about an Ex. Whatever it may be, choose to block it out. That early morning routine time is yours. Stop letting one or two things ruin your whole freaking day. Stay in the moment. Like a sacred temple but guarded by 1,000 samurai. You are self-empowered; these petty things will not disrupt your flow. You got this! Solid like a tree, you will not falter.

Mix It Up

I challenge you to mix up every routine and habit for a week. About six months ago I decided to mix everything up. The moment I woke up, made my bed different. Decided to brush my teeth while using the toilet (time management). Brushed my beard while telling myself how grateful I am for ALL I have. And much more! Sounds redundant and common sense. We're always multitasking, right? But the key for me was fine tuning some simple habits, making them more efficient so I can free up more time for daily creative projects (writing, combing through acting auditions, exercising, and leisure time). My point is that my one-week challenge to mix everything up has been going on since that day. Also, ask some of your friends you deem as successful what their morning routine and daily routine are like.

BreakFAST

It is called breakfast because you break the fasting during the sleep hours. A lot of Americans will eat a big high calorie, high carb. breakfast and their insulin levels spike. They don't burn if off and pack on the pounds. I loss 10 lbs. in 2 months by delaying my breakfast fix. Getting up at 6am and not eating anything until about 9 or 10am. Your metabolism is firing up and getting into gear. I do drink coffee the moment I'm awake or I turn into an ancient demon who's name we do not speak of. ▯

Limitations

The key to time management and over all organization is putting limitations on things. Recognize when you are spending too much time on a task. When I text with my band mate about music stuff, it is not abnormal that the texts will be long. I prefer a phone chat to put limitations on potential unnecessary text chains. I also limit this time because it's value to my life is at a hobby level or leisure activity. Don't get me wrong music is much more than that to me: it is a culture, artistic expression, and a necessary element in my life. It's just that right now it brings me very little passive income.

Metrics is not just for Nerds.

When the pandemic broke out, I was already wanting to mix up my schedule. I had no idea how much it would change. I embraced it and started fine tuning my daily habits. For example, I wanted to tighten down on my customer service day job schedule. Optimize my schedule to be more efficient and reduce anxiety about being late. Or worse than that, working longer hours. Work smart, not hard.

Put your nose to the grindstone is a dated philosophy and puts you on the fast track to burn out and poor health. So, I started setting alarms on my phone to go off: 15 minutes before my work shift, 5 minutes before my lunch, 5 minutes before my lunch break ends, and 5 minutes before the end of my shift. Big life hack here: don't look at the clock. Stay in the moment. You will become a Zen office worker. Like being on vacation, do you ever clock watch? Your answer is: heck no! And of course, your Miami South beach vacation goes by in a blink of an eye, right? Warning: the only side effect is the days go by even faster. Life goes fast.

When I was in high school, St. Edward (Catholic college preparatory), there was two weeks left before graduation. I had the task of leading prayer that morning in class. I put my hands together and said, "Please Jesus, make these next two weeks go by FAST!" The class snickered and the teacher ran over to my desk and reprimanded me. "Never wish your life away man!!!" That was 26 years ago, and those words still echo in my dome. Life is short, life is precious. Re-read those words again please.

Meditation

Meditation is key. It is the opposite extreme of the busy hustle. I think a lot of people that do not practice it, perceive it as a singularity. It is physical and mental. Try it and you'll realize you can't sit still, or your mind wonders from one subject, task, or you're anxious. Run your computer or Xbox for 5 days straight nonstop and listen to the fan going on over drive. This is your brain and your body needing to find its Zen time. Balance is key. Take a deep breath right now. You can train your brain to reprogram itself and anxiety and stress will be less.

I've been teaching myself to meditate while working my customer service job. For example, when I say my greeting over the phone, "Technical Support, my name is Ryan. How can I help you?" I first take a deep breath and exhale into my intro. My happy place is an ocean beach. I sometimes imagine my exhale is the calm ocean wave receding back to sea. If you suffer from anxiety, techniques like these will change your life and once you practice it enough it will become second nature. The goal is to avoid western medicine's toxic mind-bending drugs, antidepressants. I have never tried them and never will. I have witnessed more than one artist friend take them over the years and witnessed their creative flow abruptly stop like a bent garden house.

Zen in ALL Things

The last 6 months I have been meditating so much, it's becoming habitual that under stress or anxiety I relax into a Zen like state. We sometimes default a setting where we fight against the Universe. But what we're just actually fighting ourselves. I took a few Aikido classes in college and it amazed me how just one side step could change the situation. Yielding to the assault. Same goes with a level head and making quick focused decisions that save you time and make the best out of a tough situation. Yield to the negative. Learn from it and you become stronger.

Stay Positive

Negativity is a virus. Highly contagious and fast spreading. The cure is the opposite, a positive mind set. Sometimes positive framing seems a bit too fake or wishy washy but it's a game changer if you work in customer service or any semi toxic work environment. If you handle complaint resolution or any type of irate person for a living then this especially for you. You're not a machine. If you match that negative energy day in and day out, it will slowly drain your soul. I like to look forward to my next travel adventure or check in with a friend of similar mind set. If you don't have a friend or two like that I would suggest a roster change or upgrade. Birds of a feather, flock together.

Listen to the Universe

Recognize when you are trying to force things. The Universe will guide you. We spend so much time stuck in resistance. I think it's taken me most of my adult life to realize this. Once you are off "auto pilot" and truly mindful of your actions, clarity will illuminate your being. And you will see things are much simpler than you realize, and the Universe is on your side. Take a camping trip. Get back to nature. It will help reset your mind and cleanse it of the complications the hustle and grind of chasing money has caused.

Friends

Friends will come and go in your life. I try not to dwell on it. I have a core of friends from different chapters of my life that I have deep connections with. We reconnect once a year or so. Then in my inner circle I just have time for a few friends. These friends are my "ride or die." They should be ones you trust with your life and are positive souls and like-minded individuals. When you surround yourself with people that build you up but at the same time keep it real, then you found the right ones.

Three Deep Breathes.

Feeling anxious? Nervous? Take three deep breathes. The rush of oxygen on your brain will help ease stress and relax your muscles. I learned this in an acting class a while back. Before going on camera, if I'm nervous I do this. I do it so much now it's muscle memory. Simple game changer for any situation.

The Balance of Extremes.

Life is nothing more than balancing and managing extremes. Example, too much leisure time like playing video games or sitting at a bar every taco Tuesday will take away from your potential. I was guilty of this for years! I still play video games but set a timer. One-hour max on a weekday. On the weekend I'm a bit more liberal. On the other hand, not getting any leisure time will put you on the fast track to burn out city. Recognize what is out of balance and adjust. I like to write down 2 or 3 goals or objectives for the day. Check them off the next day and if miss one have it roll over to the new day or reschedule it.

Learn Survival Skills.

Over the years I've always been fascinated with survival skills. Fishing, fire-making, and martial arts have been a lifelong enjoyment. In the summer of 2019 when I bought a new house I made my cellar into a doomsday prepper room. All the essentials and more. Camping gear, multi-tools, basic medicines, and survival equipment. Then the pandemic hit, and I decided to upgrade it to non-perishable food storage. My point of this section is a few things: it will make you a more well-rounded individual and appreciate the modern amenities you work hard to pay for. It will also help ease your mind when or if society collapses. With climate crisis quickly getting worse and WW3 breaking out and/or waves of mutating viruses, I think being a prepper is not such a cultist or wacky thing anymore.

From doomsday prepping I have learned to be even more efficient with multi-tasking. A good prepper's actions generally serve two purposes. For example, my food cache obviously serves the purpose of having enough food in case society collapses and store shelves are empty. We saw it happen in April of 2020. The other purpose is always having meals available. I wanted to invest heavy but at the same time had a slew of bills come in. Cash flow was tight for Uber Eats, so mac and cheese it is.

If you're not sure about where to start, take a primitive camping trip. Watch YouTube videos on specific survival skills like fire-making and then go and apply it. Funny how a single oily corn chip in your pocket can be an excellent fire-starting source.

Travel!

There is nothing like discovering a new park or museum or a beach! The last 10 years I have travelled all over the U.S. for film work and leisure. There is no greater education then travel. You really learn the culture of each city and region. And you meet lots of strangers that will teach you more and give you an individual's perspective that may totally change your opinion of a city or region. If more people travelled and got out of their bubble the world be more caring and understanding. But the point of this section and this handbook is for you to be more skilled and open minded too. Use budget airlines and ARBN to stretch your dollar. The world is waiting out there to be your professor. Like nature it will teach you the good and the bad with no filters. The bad experiences will be your greatest life lessons.

Procrastination is Your Dream Killer.

About 6 months ago I realized how much I procrastinate. It was really holding me back. Having cut down on boozing and not spending so much time sitting in bars wasting away, suddenly I have all this free time. I started making lists. Project lists for my new house and goals for my passions: acting, writing, and travelling. I'm very visible. I have this project list taped to my home office wall. I put a line through each one when complete. Other lists include a credit card bill that documents the current balance and each payment that is dated. On a personal note I have two photos on the same wall of my Grandfathers in uniform their U.S. Army uniforms. Both just back from their tours during WWII. On my worst day at my day job, nothing compares to what they went through. I need to add another photo of my father, also Army. Served in Vietnam. #RyanRant. Anyway, be mindful of your procrastinations and spear head them. You will feel rewarded by crossing off tasks and achieving goals. Success will follow.

Mantra

Daily mantra is in many forms. Soon as I wake up I tell my cat, Raul, let's get up and do something fun! Animals respond to your energy and the big fur ball jumps up and is ready for adventure. Lol. I also use mantra during my pre-hockey game warm up (I play in a men's recreational ice hockey league). After stretching I meditate. I repeat to myself my body is made of steel and my mind flows like water. I'm laser focused.

Porn = the Death of your Relationship

By watching pornography while in a relationship you rewire your brain. You condition it. "I can't compete with that." Says every girlfriend ever! It's true. Not just that your male brain is processing nonstop mostly unimaginable sexual situations but it's also training your brain to only respond to perfect 10 models. That's all I'm going to write on this topic. There are many books about it to take it further.

Exercise More

For my day job I sit at a desk in my home office. My commute is seven steps. I noticed in the last three years my health has declined. And about three years ago is when I started to work from home. So here is an example of the balance of extremes. I sit all day so for the last three months I walk before work, on my lunch break, and after my shift is over. Averaging about 5 miles a day. Now I sleep better and feel healthier. Find your routine and don't forget to let your body heal. 5 miles a day in just two weeks is 70 miles!

Stand Guard of Your Mind.

Imagine you are the emperor of your mind. You have a legion of a thousand samurai that protect it. No single thought, negative situation, nor insult can infiltrate that palace of your mind. The samurai protect it and stand guard. My point. Be careful who you let it. I'm not saying to be paranoid but recognize when someone or something is not healthy for your mind or trying to disrupt the harmony of your kingdom. If I had a time machine I would go back and tell my past self not to trust so many people and let them in to my most personal thoughts and past experiences.

Envision Success

Just like a pro athlete's ritual before a game, envision your success. What are the specific things you need to do? As an actor, before I get on camera and do a scene. I envision my performance. Rehearse it in my mind. When I was fifteen years old I made a stage in my basement for all our band equipment. My drums, my band mate's guitars and amps. I situated lights shining on the equipment. I dreamed of being a rockstar and playing on big stages. That dream took about ten years, but it happened! I accomplished everything I could imagine. We got on small record labels, toured, played some big venues, and are still making some royalty money many years later. Anyway, dream it and practice your craft. You can accomplish great things!

Stop Worrying...

Stop worrying about the things you can't control. Just as people tend to dwell on past mistakes, they absorb a ton of time worrying about the future. I'm not saying don't reflect on past mistakes. We gain insight when we reflect on a past relationship and by doing so might not repeat the same mistakes. But stop worrying so much. It's OK to be concerned about the future but if you're doing things like getting out of debt, investing in yourself, and surrounding yourself with positive genuine people, the future will be rewarding. If you try to sail a boat with the anchor down, the journey will be extra tedious and taxing on the boat. That anchor is negative thoughts and fear of what lies ahead. Let it go! Stay positive and sail on!

What Doesn't Destroy You…

What doesn't destroy you makes you stronger. Cliché right? But it's so true. Your biggest strengths will come from your biggest failures. Embrace them. Learn and adjust. If negative things didn't happen to good people there would be oblivion. It is the harmony within the disharmony. Ying and yang.

To Do Lists

I have four sets of to do lists. On one wall in my office I have a dry erase board that is for my art projects (acting goals and video content). My second list is on another wall and that one is all about long term things like home projects and debt pay offs. My third list is a daily one. I write about 2 or 3 objectives/goals for each day in my notebook next to me in my office. I put today's date on it like a journal. Then I have a monthly list of bills. Each with a box next to it. When I pay it, I put an "X" in the box. Also, I write one word that describes the mood or tone I want to set for the month. For example, September "Focus". I recently started an online sales course and between that and writing this book, I'm getting a lot of academic time in. Taking breaks for long walks by the lake and zoning out is the balance.

Learning to Let Go.

I think I could write a book solely about this chapter. Recognize what you keep fighting against and let it go. I got married young and had a wonderful caring wife. I didn't realize how amazing she was until many years later. For years I kicked myself for leaving such a great soul. Eventually I let it go. Eventually you must forgive yourself. I think when I did this it gave closure and truly ended that chapter in my life. Recognize things that are pulling you back in the past. Sever that emotional baggage and live for today.

READ More.

Did you know the average CEO reads about 5 books a month? Mama mia! The last six months I've read about 6 books. Lately, I'm only reading entrepreneur books and averaging about one a week! Such a game changer. I feel like my brain is firing on all cylinders! And using Amazon Kindle is cost effective, I get the book immediately, and it's green friendly (Amazon is not paying me to say that.) ▯

Check Your Ego at the Door Please!

This is one of the best lessons I learned in my acting studies. Especially working with fellow artists it's important to practice this and recognize when you might be letting yours get in the way. Once you check your ego at the door then you can really work as a team. Try it the next board meeting in business or be up front and tell the team to do so. Watch what a difference this friendly reminder can make. The focus on the art itself will be stronger or the business objective at hand.

Learn to "Shelf it."

Sometimes we want to accomplish a task or goal so bad after a while its counterproductive. Like the old saying trying to fit a round hole in a square peg. Shelf it. Then circle back to it a few hours later or the next day with a fresh perspective. You'll be amazed how more productive you will be.

Path of Least Resistance.

In high school I was called lazy by my teachers and my parents. I felt like a prisoner in school (Catholic school) and didn't have any motivation to be some honor student. Now as an adult I recognize what is worth my time (again our most valuable asset) and take the path of least resistance. I'll get more into this in the next few chapters. I think they are the most important. A combination of standing guard of your mind and time management.

Work vs. Leisure Time.

For the last 21 years as a technical rep. for a Fortune 500 company the following quote has been taped to my PC monitor: "Work like you'll live forever. Play like you will die tomorrow." – Charles Fleming. Another balance of extremes. The hustle is real so should your leisure time. The past 4 months I used my vacation time to take half day Friday's off. Working 8am until 12 noon for a longer weekend during summer our busiest season. A game changer for my happiness. And my numbers are the best ever. A happy employee equals a productive one! Also, take mini vacations. I found this primitive cabin only an hour away as an easy escape. Cost effective Arbnb made it affordable to get away any weekend I wanted to.

High School Emotional Maturity.

It took me about 40 years to realize that the average person's emotionally maturity level doesn't go past high school! Once you realize this you'll stop wasting your time on these people. They break all the rules, like the chapters in this handbook and having a debate with them is futile. Stand guard of your mind and respect your sanity by avoiding them. Make a list right now of people in your workplace, Facebook friends, and family. I bet a lot of them are at this level. It's sad but true.

The Slider, The Platea-er, & The Great Climber.

There are three types of people on the spinning ball of rock in space: The Slider is one who slowly slides through life. Mainly backwards and has very little care about themselves, their actions, and about others. Or they just care about themselves and are dishonest to themselves and others. The Platea-er is most people. They've settled. They are not interested in taking risks but want to feel safe and spend way too much time concerned about what others think. The Great Climber is one who cares about others, the planet, innovation, progression, and is highly motivated. A great risk taker and leader. Which one are you?

Stop Arguing with Stupid People

Especially on social media. Once you enter their arena of stupidity and try to use the voice of reason, you're lowering your own IQ and devaluing your time. You will not reach them, only waste your time and ruin your calm.

How to be Your Own Doctor

You're smarter than you think. And you probably know your body better than a western medicine doctor. He or she is really a legal drug dealer/ pharmaceutical salesperson. I'm not saying to never go to the doctor but first do research and then go if you must. I healed myself with Chinese herbs I took for a year. I mentioned in the preface finding out I had three tumors on my spleen. I did research online and read up on it. I ordered the herbs on Amazon and now I'm fine. The herbs treated the source vs. going under the knife.

Do What Makes Your Soul Sing.

For me being a musician has been my heart and soul. Playing the drums, bass, or guitar make my soul sing. What makes your soul sing? Maybe it's camping or a walk on the beach. Whatever it is do it more often. About once a year I drive 10 hours to Virginia Beach to spent time walking on the boardwalk, watching the ocean waves, and eating fresh crab legs. I'm getting ready to go in a few days. Much needed time away after quarantine because of the pandemic. It won't be all leisure though. I'm currently taking an online sales class. That will go with me on my labtop and I'll be doing a brand ambassador photo shoot for a beard company. Nice balance of leisure and hustle! This makes my soul sing too.

Take an Acting Class.

This was a real game changer for me. I took theater acting classes in college but later in life started taking film acting classes. It changed my life in so many ways. I was kind of a shy kid growing up. It's a classic tale of a bashful kid projecting a character that is the opposite, confident or boisterous. After a while it becomes second nature when you want to portray that confidence. It will enhance how you speak, your posture, improve your listening skills, and more. Be sure to get a copy of my book "On Camera Experience 101" also available on Amazon! ⏎

Stop Comparing Yourself to Others.

This is part of the high school emotional maturity. You do you. Focus on your path and what makes you happy. People want more and more and are not satisfied unless they have a bigger house then yours or nicer clothes, cars, etc. I don't want what they have.

Honestly, I had it before. House, sports car, and a truck. I was never truly happy. I wanted what others had. About 6 years ago I traded in my BMW for a Fiat. It gets 61 miles to the gallon on the highway. "This little car, takes me far." Is my mantra on long road trips while I'm cramped inside it. But it's worth the tradeoff. Super cost effective!

No Excuses.

This is probably the most important chapter in this handbook. I can't stress it enough. No excuses. It's amazing how many excuses we'll make a day to validate not completing daily chores or a life changing career change. In studying acting and film making this practice is crucial! Just like checking your ego at the door, no excuses are just as important. It's a tough challenge but once we are mindful of it we'll catch ourselves making an excuse, adjust, and execute the solution.

Recognize and Stop Distractions.

There is nothing worse than having your creative flow constantly interrupted by social media or texts. First I started with "Silent Sundays." Silencing my phone for the day to take a break from always being connected. Audition notices, investing subscriptions, and more constantly demanding me time. The last few weeks I switched that to every day. Silence. Such a game changer. Of course, you can adjust your phone's notifications (and I do that) but having zero phone distractions is key to staying focus. Schedule time at lunch or in the evening for 30 or 60 minutes to answer texts or emails.

Cut Off Toxic People!

I started doing this about 4 years ago and what a game changer. "Birds of a feather flock together." Friends or family it doesn't matter. Your environment and people in it should be healthy and progressive. Again, like sailing a ship pulling an anchor. It may sink the ship. Why carry their toxic burden with you? Life is too short. You can't evolve in a toxic pool filled with people that will bring you down with them.

Show Them, Don't Tell Them.

This is one I wish I learned 10 years ago but there is no time like the present. In any career especially the entertainment industry it's easy to get caught up in the excitement of what you plan on achieving. But show them, don't tell them. You can talk about being successful all you want but the results speak for themselves. Everything else is just hearsay.

Watch More Documentaries

One that changed my life is called "The Minimalists." Physical things in your life you buy actually own you. Less is more. I donated clothes and had yard sales to minimalize my life. I feel more in control of it and it's just easier to clean and organize.

A Smoothie a Day!

What a game changer. A smoothie a day the last 6 months has improved my mind, body, and soul! Adding fruits and vegetables with coconut milk has given me more energy and a positive mind set. Especially kale, a super food! I got my single glass smoothie mixer for about $30 on Amazon, so they're not that expensive. No excuses. Get one and a healthier lifestyle will follow. My refrigerator used to be packed with beer and now it's vegetables, super green dry mix, flaxseed, beats, and more!

Recognize your Addictions!

Addictions are in many forms. My biggest one was binge drinking. You may not realize it until you get sick like I did. Taco Tuesday, thirsty Thursdays, Friday happy hours, Saturday nights, and Sunday Fundays. That leaves you with Monday and Wednesday just two days of the week sober. Once I stopped this toxic schedule and controlled my alcohol addiction my life changed. The focus on reading, writing, exercise, and meditation. Let's not forget sugar and caffeine are other forms of addiction. I think sugar is the biggest one! I'm not saying stop drinking but find balance. I've limited myself to three drinks and for the last six months it's been red wines. Antioxidants, not too shabby!

Power Naps.

I think we spend more time charging our smart phones then ourselves. One 15-minute power nap a day is a game changer for me. I put on meditation music. Brain wave music. It's brief but a perfect little recharge.

Use apps for Time Management

Time is your most valuable asset. First I started using an app called TODY to organize my chores, then I started using it to organize my workout routines, doctor appointments, home improvement projects, and reminders to brush my cat or give him his flea meds. It almost makes doing chores fun and it's free. A clean organized house is a clean organized life! I also use an app called, Calm, for meditation exercises, Downward Dog for Yoga, and Pacer to keep track of my daily miles for walking/jogging.

Decision Making: + and – T chart.

Have a hard time making decisions? Take a piece of paper and draw a T. Positives on one side and the negatives on the other. It's nice because it is visual and quite frankly if one side is greater than the other then there's your answer. I've used this many times when trying to decide if a relationship was working out with a girlfriend. Especially when it comes to the matters of the heart, we want to be decisive.

Stop Clock Watch at your 9 to 5 Job

As I mentioned in a previous chapter, I started using metrics to better organize my 9 to 5 job. I use various alarms set on my phone. I have an alarm that goes off 15 minutes before my shift starts so I'm always on time. Another goes off 5 minutes before my lunch break starts. Another 5 minutes at the end of my lunch, so I'm on time when I go back. And then a last one that goes off 5 minutes before my shift ends. I don't look at the clock at all. So, I'm in the zone and focused. Very Zen. The downside is time goes by very fast, almost too fast. Life is short and precious, never wish your life away!

Wake up 3 hours before the day job.

Rise and grind they say. I don't think so. You want to ease into the day. Ease into the grind. All the best entrepreneurs and successful businesspeople are up early in the gym or out jogging. I say besides the health benefits of exercise you also need valuable "me time." I go to bed around 10pm and I'm up at 6am. I'll do one or two chores, walk outside, drink a half a glass of water, read the Wall Street Journal, and write down my three goals or tasks for the day. I also review yesterday's goals/tasks and make sure I achieved them. Again, the secret to your success is in the daily routine.

Daily practice of Mind, Body, Soul.

In the last 6 months doing these simple daily practices have changed my life. And my stats for my day job are the best in 21 years! Reading the newspaper and self-improvement books (MIND). Stretching and walking about 5 miles a day (BODY). And meditation

(SOUL). Envision success and believe in yourself so strong you will start to carry that confidence with you every day and achieve great things.

Recognize when you need Mini Breaks from the Hustle.

No one wants to burn out, but it happens often. Recognize when you need a vacation or at least a break from non-stop scheduling. I was recently on a 4-day vacation in Virginia Beach. I took my laptop for an online sales class I'm taking and a book I'm reading/studying about entrepreneurship. When I got settled in at my ocean front hotel, I realized that I needed more breaks from both. Long walks on the boardwalk and relaxing seafood meals was the perfect recipe for decompression time. After the 4 days I felt rejuvenated and ready to get back to the hustle! Hit the reset button every now and then.

The Haters: Kill them with Kindness.

"As the love for you grows, so does the hate like 3 times over!" For more about that follow this link for an interview I did a few years ago:

https://www.clevelandedits.com/blog/2017/8/18/a-glimpse-into-the-life-of-a-cleveland-actor

The haters are really fans in disguise. Your energy is too valuable. Don't give them the time of day and when confronted by their toxic vibes, kill them with kindness. Also, don't be surprised when there are haters close to you. Friends and family can get jealous and maybe they don't even realize when they are doing it to you.

Decide what you need to Sacrifice in your life to free up TIME.

In the Amazon when farmers need to cross their herd of cows over rivers, they take an old or sick cow and let it go first. When or if piranhas attack then it will be sacrificed so the herd can safely cross the river. For me the two biggest things I'm currently sacrificing is money and health. Instead of going out on weekends with friends or buying a Tesla, I'm saving money for my investments and getting out of debt. Also, focusing on being active every day so I'm healthy enough to see my investment returns! Decide what you need to sacrifice, especially if you feel like you don't have enough time or money to accomplish your dreams.

Have a "spa day."

Cleanse and relax the body, calm the mind, and your soul will sing you praise. I try to do this at least once a year. A day devoted to healing, meditation, relaxation, and most importantly, detoxification. You don't have to spend money on a real spa. Take a hot bath with Epsom salt. Soak your feet. Get the toxins out. Drink lots of cucumber water. Use a rolling pin to get the lactic acid out of your weary legs and arms. I use the rolling pin daily and especially the day after a hockey game or long hike.

The Lazy Investor Portfolio

Two years ago, I started a Robinhood brokerage account with $50. It is currently worth $4,463 and in the last year I am up 14.77%. I encourage you to do the same. There are different types of investing strategies. Mine is a slow building one but with less risk. I buy shares of Apple, Coka-Cola, and real estate ETFs that pay decent dividends. I use DRIPS aka dividend reinvestment programs. Meaning once I'm paid for a dividend it automatically goes back into buy more shares of that company. So, it's hands off passive income. Set it and forget it is what they say. Each pay day I put about $100 to $200 into my Robinhood account. Last night while I was sleeping I was making money. Woke up at 3:30am to the following dividends received and will be reinvested the next day: FCPT (real estate) $2.16, DEI (real estate) $.57, O (real estate) $1.42, ERIC (5G) $.33, IIPR (cannabis real estate for greenhouses) $2.37, and more!

Set Strict Deadlines

You will be surprised how much you can accomplish in a short amount of time. For my 9 to 5 job I need to be on the phones answering calls as much as possible. If I'm doing an off the phone task, I set a timer for 5 minutes. I accomplish tasks faster and a lot of times there is time left over.

Stop Waiting in Lines

Outsource that work to save time. Your time is too precious. I use an app called Instacart. So, while I'm working and being productive, someone else is standing in line. And the app lists all products on sale so you can still be frugal.

Compete with Yourself not with Friends nor Family.

I think it's hard to do. You catch yourself at times competing with ones dear to you. I haven't for a very long time, and I feel balanced. You must tune them out. The only way you will tap into your true potential is being your biggest critic and each day competing with yourself. How do I improve today so tomorrow I'm better?

Mix Things Up.

Mix up your routine and other things. I mean everything. From your morning routine to what you wear to bed – to how you brush your teeth, what you read, eat, drink, how you laugh, clothes, etc. I tried it one day and then it turned into months! It gives you perspective on your own habits and what you can improve. I think we can all agree that the pandemic certainly forced us to mix things up. Embrace change and redesign your routine.

Beware of FEAR and GREED.

The two biggest elements that fuel the stock market are fear and greed. But in your everyday life they can control you and hurt your productivity and life. Ask yourself if a decision you are about to make is from a place of fear or a place of knowledge. Be mindful of your greed. Do you really need a brand-new car? New clothes? An expensive night on the town for dinner and drinks? Stop hemorrhaging money that you could put to better use, like getting out of debt, savings, or investing in your future.

Don't Aim for the Fence, Aim for the parking lot!

Baseball analogy loading… If your goal as baseball player is to just hit the ball over the fence, you'll probably come up short or just get a base hit. It's good but you want to be great. You need to envision hitting the ball deep out of the stadium and into the parking lot. Seeing it bounce off that cement! Aim big, dream big. Think big.

Some Days You're the bug, some days you're the windshield.

About 12 years ago a customer of mine from Georgia, an older gentleman, was unhappy with the outcome of our conversation but realized he was in the wrong. At the end of the call he told me "Son, somedays you're the bug and somedays you're the windshield. Today I screwed up and I got squished." My point is you will fail and there will be days you get squished like a bug. Don't dwell on it. It's the balance of things. This quote pops in my head on days that are just not going well. Tomorrow is a new day, be the windshield.

Pay It Back.

Remember where you came from. Who helped you stay on the right path and encouraged you to be the best version of you? Thank them. Be a mentor. Send the elevator back up. Give back to the universe. Help others evolve and spread your knowledge. Together maybe we can help culminate a better world.

The Value of Kindness and Integrity.

I'm not trying to hit you with religion nor preach but love thy neighbor. If we all treated each other like a trusted neighbor what a different world it would be. Are you the same person behind close doors as you are in the public eye? Would your ancestors be proud of how you treat others? Kindness and integrity are undervalued in our society. Just like a virus, positivity and kindness are infectious too.

Choose Your Mentors Wisely.

I have been fortunate enough to have great mentors throughout my life. Hockey teammates, karate instructors, football teammates, band mates, my parents, and friends. My latest ones for the last 6 months that have enhanced my life are entrepreneur YouTubers: Stefan James and Andrei Jihk. Both are successful businessmen and seem like all around good dudes.

Life is Like Walking on a Tight Rope.

The key is balance. Balance that starts with your daily routine. The dedication to mind, body, and soul. Distilled in the daily hustle. Remember you are not alone. Your mentors will guide you. Meditation will calm your mind, so you remain focused and diligent. Your mental army of miniature samurai will march across that tight rope keeping you from falling. Life is not a race. Why would you run across a tight rope? Remember a smoothie a day will keep the doctor away. And eat lots of raw vegetables and fruit each day. Eat in colors! Know when to take breaks, you are not a machine.

Embrace the dark times in your life. They will be your greatest life lessons. When you feel like you've fallen down a well of despair. All hope is not lost. Look up. There is a glimpse of light at the top of the well. The only place from there is to go up. Get to the light no matter what sacrifice you need to do. You will succeed. And once you get there you'll gain perspective and appreciate all you have and remember where you came from.

Remember less is more. You want to build a life where your money is working for you. Not being a slave to your money nor materialistic things living paycheck to paycheck. Invest in yourself. I challenge you to read one non-fiction book a week! I recommend: The Big Book of Income, Hustle, and The 5 Day Weekend. You got this! Tap into your true potential and success will follow.

Interested in talking about any of these chapters in more detail? Book me through my Facebook Page: "Ryan's Mind, Body, and Soul Consulting" **@ryansmindbodysoulconsulting.**